FANTASY

YOU WRITE IT!

BY
JOHN HAMILTON

Published by ABDO Publishing Company, 8000 West 78th Street, Suite 310, Edina, Minnesota 55439.

Editor: Sue Hamilton
Graphic Design: Sue Hamilton
Cover Design: Neil Klinepier
Cover Illustration: Background image, Don Maitz; Foreground image, iStock
Interior Photos and Illustrations: p 1 Fantasy art, Getty Images; p 3 Dagger, iStock; p 4 Knight, iStock; Dragon silhouette, iStock; p 5 *Lord of the Rings* still frames, courtesy New Line Cinema; p 6 Magic floating book, iStock; p 7 Index card, iStock; Boy reading, Getty Images; p 8 Girl writing, iStock; p 9 Girl with typewriter, Getty Images; p 10 Writing with quill pen, iStock; *Lord of the Rings* Gandalf still frame, courtesy New Line Cinema; p 11 Index card, iStock; p 12 Wizard, iStock; p 13 Dragon, iStock; p 14 *Conan the Barbarian* still, courtesy Universal Pictures; pp 15-16 *Lord of the Rings* still frames, courtesy New Line Cinema; p 17 Knight, Comstock; p 18 Girl in library and Post-it Note, iStock; p 19 Knight, iStock; pp 20-23 *Harry Potter and the Sorcerer's Stone* still frames, courtesy Warner Bros. Pictures; p 24 Girl cheering, iStock; p 25 Wizard art, Getty Images; p 26 *Fantasy & Science Fiction* magazine cover, courtesy Spilogale, Inc.; p 27 Mailbox with computer keyboard, Comstock; p 28 *Harry Potter and the Sorcerer's Stone* book cover, courtesy Scholastic Inc.; J.K. Rowling, AP Images; p 29 *Neverwhere*, courtesy HarperCollins; *The Hobbit,* courtesy Houghton Mifflin; p 32 Boy riding dragon, Getty Images.

Library of Congress Cataloging-in-Publication Data

Hamilton, John, 1959-
  You write it : fantasy / John Hamilton.
      p. cm. -- (You write it!)
  Includes index.
  ISBN 978-1-60453-504-4
  1. Fantasy fiction--Authorship--Juvenile literature. I. Title.

PN3377.5.F34H36 2009
808.3'8766--dc22
                                  2008042605

CONTENTS

INTRODUCTION

"Fantasy is hardly an escape from reality. It's a way of understanding it."

—Lloyd Alexander

Fantasy is one of the hottest genres in fiction. Updated for today's audiences, fantasy submerges readers in worlds filled with elves, fairies, knights, dragons, and wizards. Some of the most beloved characters in literature were born in fantasy: Harry Potter, Frodo Baggins, King Arthur, and many more.

Fantasy allows us to see the world with wonder, just like children. With all our rigid notions of science and reality set aside, fantasy helps us make sense of larger issues, like good versus evil, fate, and the ability of individuals, no matter how small, to change the world.

Fantasy sets our imaginations free. We step through a magic portal, or a looking glass, or a rabbit hole, into a new world that fills us with a sense of wonder. Legends are retold, and new tales are spun. In the magical world of fantasy, anything is possible.

Countless fantasy books, short stories, movies, and TV shows are created each year. Perhaps *you've* got a fantasy story you're dying to tell. But where to start?

Novelist Gene Fowler once said, "Writing is easy. All you do is stare at a blank sheet of paper until drops of blood form on your forehead." What he meant is that writing is much harder than it looks. Anybody who can form a simple sentence thinks they can write. But good writing, like any other skill, takes practice.

Few people are born writers. However, there are certain skills anyone can learn. These "tools of the trade" can help you master the *craft* of writing. And once you've mastered the craft, you're well on your way to writing fantasy stories that others will love. You will encounter many obstacles along the way, but good writers find a way. The important thing is persistence, and a burning desire to tell your story.

Setting

At the heart of fantasy is a journey. It is an adventure that travels from a familiar place, like home, to an unknown, evil place, and then returns. The subtitle of J.R.R. Tolkien's *The Hobbit* says it all: *There and Back Again*. Think carefully as you construct your story's setting. Your hero and villain each have distinct personalities. So, too, should your familiar place and evil place. Think of these places as characters. In Tolkien's *The Lord of the Rings*, the familiar place was the reassuring Shire, the fertile land of the peace-loving hobbits. Contrast the Shire to the story's evil place, the frightful land of Mordor, with its oppressive swamps and deserts and black-walled castles.

Top and Bottom: In *The Lord of the Rings*, there is a sharp contrast between the beauty of the Shire and the dark evil of Mordor.

IDEAS

"The main way to get started as a writer is to write: apply the seat of the pants firmly to the seat of the chair and just get down to it. Having a thousand "good ideas" in your head is no good; you have to get them on paper. Just sit down and do it."

—Marion Zimmer Bradley

The number one question asked of many fantasy writers is, where do you get your ideas? It's usually asked by insecure beginners who are afraid they don't have the imagination it takes to be successful. But as you'll soon find out, ideas are everywhere: in your head, in a book of fairy tales, in a stray conversation overheard at lunch. Developing an idea into a *story* is where the hard work takes place.

Many fantasy stories have their roots in ancient myths and folktales. Some of the characters and creatures of J.K. Rowling's Harry Potter books are variations of creatures found in English folklore. J.R.R. Tolkien borrowed heavily from Norse mythology to get ideas for his Middle-earth books.

To get ideas for your own stories, find books that retell folktales and myths. Many fantasy stories are centered in medieval Europe, but remember that the rest of the world is also rich with folklore, which can be mined by creative writers. Perhaps your story is a twist on Japanese folklore, or the mythology of the ancient Mayas or Aztecs. And don't overlook the wildly creative story traditions of ancient Africa.

Popular Fantasy Categories

High Fantasy—Tales of medieval kingdoms battling evil forces. Filled with wizards, knights, kings and queens. Examples: *Lord of the Rings, Narnia.*

Adventure Fantasy—Exciting adventures, sometimes called "sword and sorcery" stories. Smaller tales centered on fewer characters, but filled with barbarian hoards, dragons, and witches. Examples: *Conan the Barbarian, The Wizard of Oz.*

Fairy Tales—Small but dramatic stories that use magic and fantasy to teach moral lessons. Examples: *Beauty and the Beast, Snow White.*

Coming Up With Ideas

- You must *read* in order to write. This is especially true with fantasy fiction. Read a lot. Every day.

- Write what you know. Use your past experiences, then translate them into ideas.

- Brainstorm! Time yourself for two minutes. Jot down any ideas that pop into your head. Don't edit yourself, even if you think the ideas are stupid. They may spark even more creativity later.

- Keep a daily journal. It can be a diary or a blog, but it can also include ideas that pop into your head, drawings, articles, photos, etc. As you collect information, you'll see patterns begin to emerge of things that interest you the most. Explore these themes.

- Write down your dreams. And your daydreams.

WORK HABITS

"Work every day. No matter what has happened the day or night before, get up and bite on the nail."
—Ernest Hemingway

Established writers will tell you over and over, the only way to learn to write is to write every day. It bears repeating: write… every… day. You wouldn't hire a carpenter to build your house unless he or she had a lot of practice in the craft, right? Do you think Michael Phelps broke swimming speed records the first time he jumped in a pool? Of course not! He spent thousands of hours in the water refining and perfecting his technique before he won his first gold medal. Writing is like any other craft or sport: it takes practice.

Find your own special place to write, a place where you can work uninterrupted. You can't wait for the mood to strike. You have to make time, even if you're busy. J.K. Rowling famously wrote much of *Harry Potter and the Sorcerer's Stone* in neighborhood cafes. (Her baby fell asleep during walks, so she ducked into cafes to take advantage of precious writing time.) If you have a laptop, you might think you can write anywhere. But it's usually best to find a single place to write. A desk in your bedroom might do, especially if you can close the door.

Or maybe a corner table in the library, or a quiet nook in a coffee shop. Think of it as your home base. Psychologically, it will help you tune out the world and get down to the business of writing.

Friends and family can be a terrible distraction. Even a minor interruption can stall your creativity. Enlist their help by making clear to them that you need to be left alone during your writing time. It doesn't always work, of course. But as you become a more practiced writer, it will take you less and less time to recover from life's inevitable distractions.

Don't Plagiarize

Writers are creative people. They want to bring their own ideas to life and share them with the world. Sometimes, though, deadline pressure (or sheer laziness) causes people to plagiarize others' work. Stealing somebody else's writing is a terrible idea. Not only is it totally wrong, it can bring you serious trouble. You can be suspended from school, expelled from college, or fired from a job. Don't do it! Besides, the world wants to read what springs from *your* mind, not somebody else's.

Right: Write what comes to your creative mind.

CHARACTER CREATION

"First, find out what your hero wants, then just follow him!"
—Ray Bradbury

What's more important, plot or character? Some writers say plot. After all, your readers are expecting a good story. On the other hand, think of the best books you've ever read. Chances are, what you remember most are the interesting characters, like Harry Potter, Gandalf the wizard, or King Arthur.

The truth is, both elements are critical to good storytelling. You can't have one without the other. The reason characters are so memorable is because they are the key to unlocking the emotions of your story. You empathize with them, feel what they feel. Through great characters, you have an emotional stake in the outcome of the story. If you don't care about the characters, why should you care how the story turns out?

Right: Gandalf is an important character in *Lord of the Rings*.

Character Biographies

Good writers are people watchers. Study the people you meet every day. Start a character journal; write down what makes these people interesting to you. Observe their physical characteristics and their behavior. What quirks do they have? How do they dress? How do they walk and talk? Mold and twist these traits into your own fictional characters.

Many writers find it helpful to create very detailed biographies of all their major characters. This sometimes helps you to discover your characters' strengths and weaknesses, which you can use later when you throw them into the boiling stew of your plot.

Backstory is the history you create for your characters. Most of it may never make it into your final draft, but it helps make your characters seem more "real" as you write.

Character Biography Checklist

Below is a list of traits you might want to consider for each of your characters. You should at least know this backstory information for your hero and main villain. What other traits can you think of that will round out your characters' biographies?

Character Biography Checklist

✓ Character's full name
✓ Nickname
✓ Age/Birthdate
✓ Color of eyes/hair
✓ Height/weight
✓ Ethnic background
✓ Physical imperfections
✓ Glasses/contacts
✓ Family background
✓ Spouse/children
✓ Religion
✓ Politics
✓ School
✓ Special skills
✓ Military
✓ Job/profession
✓ Hobbies/sports
✓ Bad habits
✓ Fears
✓ Hopes and dreams

Character is Action

Characters are revealed through their actions. Instead of telling us that a knight is brave, show him rescuing a helpless child from a pack of goblins. Don't say that a wizard is powerful; show him waving a wand and turning an orc into a mouse. The point is, it's always better to reveal your characters' personalities through their behavior. Let their actions speak for themselves. It's one of the basic rules of fiction: show, don't tell!

Viewpoint

Whose "voice" is telling your story? The vast majority of fiction uses one of two viewpoints: first person and third person. First-person viewpoint uses the "I" voice, as if the reader were experiencing the action personally. For example: *I was in the presence of royalty. Here before me was a leader of men, a mighty warrior the likes of which the world had never before seen. But why, I wondered, was he so scrawny?* First-person can be used very effectively to inhabit the thoughts and feelings of your main character. However, in first person your readers know only what your main character knows. This can sometimes limit your book, unless you are a very skilled storyteller.

On the other hand, third-person viewpoint (often called "third-person omniscient," or "the eye of God") lets you describe things your main character might not be aware of. You can describe your characters' feelings, but you can also take a step back and view the action from a more distant, neutral viewpoint.

For example: *The dragon had two blazing red eyes, and nostrils that billowed smoke. Shiny scales glittered in the sunlight, dazzling to the eye. Two great, bat-like wings spread out on either side of the massive red body. The dragon uncoiled its neck and moved its head down to Charlie's eye level. All the boy could do was crouch there, petrified, as the beast sniffed him, snorting and huffing like some nightmare locomotive. A set of enormous teeth, white as ivory, gnashed up and down. Gobs of drool spilled over a jawbone that was as long as Charlie was tall.* For beginning writers, third-person viewpoint is a good choice. It has fewer pitfalls and complications.

Short stories almost always use a single viewpoint throughout. In longer forms, like novels, some authors like to mix up viewpoints for variety. Varying viewpoints can be very entertaining, but remember to keep the same viewpoint in each scene. Otherwise, you'll confuse your reader.

Heroes

Your hero is your main character, or protagonist. He or she is the person the story is about. It's through the hero that your readers experience your story, and make an emotional connection with the other characters.

In most high-fantasy stories, the hero begins as an ordinary peasant, or perhaps an unremarkable prince in a peaceable kingdom. Then some sort of menace, a creeping unknown, threatens the land. The hero sets off on an adventure. Along the way, he learns magic and fighting skills, and also something about the nature of good versus evil. After conquering the evil, the hero returns home, wiser, and perhaps with a treasure to share.

In fantasy adventure stories, the Conan-type of sword-and-sorcery tales, the heroes are built a little differently. Right from the start,

Above: Conan-type heroes are ready for action right away.

these vigorous warriors are ready-made for action. These stories are less about lessons learned than about using one's wits and skills to overcome great odds.

Whatever kind of hero you choose, keep in mind one important thing: he or she should be likable. Fantasy readers will quickly abandon your book if your hero is disagreeable.

To make your hero likeable, make him or her a capable person. The hero should be competent enough to complete the quest on his own, without calling in the cavalry. Give him a likeable trait or two. And be sure to give him a personal stake in the story. The reader will be much more engaged if the hero is personally threatened by the villain in some way.

Also, don't forget to give your heroes some flaws to overcome. This makes them seem more human, and interesting. Readers will root for a hero if they can relate to their fears and insecurities.

The Villain

The villain is the antagonist of the story, the one who tries to keep your hero from accomplishing his or her goal. Villains can be great fun to write. Many villains in fantasy stories are pure evil, since the point of these tales is the struggle of good versus evil. Think of Sauron in *The Lord of the Rings*. But the most effective villains, especially in fantasy adventures, have weaknesses and motivations we can relate to. Nobody's afraid of a villain who's all bluster and anger. But create a villain who seems like someone we could bump into on the street, and you've created something special.

An effective technique is to make your villains charming. It's what the villains use to lure their innocent victims, including your readers. Charming villains are villains we love to hate.

The Lord of the Rings included Saruman, the evil wizard (*above*), and the chief villain, Sauron (*right*).

Secondary Characters

Fantasy stories are almost always populated by a rich variety of secondary characters. They are critical in helping your hero overcome the problems you throw in his way. Many types of secondary characters show up again and again in stories. Joseph Campbell, the great scholar of mythology, identified many characters who have common purposes. He called them archetypes, a kind of common personality trait first identified by psychologist Carl Jung.

A *mentor*, or "wise old man or woman," gives critical help or knowledge to the hero. An obvious mentor character in *The Lord of the Rings* is the wizard Gandalf, who helps Frodo and his band of adventurers along their way to Mount Doom.

Threshold guardians, also called gatekeeper guardians, are characters who block the hero along the way. Threshold guardians test the hero, preparing him to battle the main villain later in the story. In fantasy stories, minions of the main villain, like orcs, make good threshold guardians.

Tricksters are helper characters who can be mischievous even as they assist the hero. Sometimes these characters are sidekicks who provide comic relief in contrast to the serious hero. A story that is serious all the time can be exhausting to read. Tricksters can help lighten the mood between dramatic scenes. Merry Brandybuck and Pippin Took often played the part of tricksters in *The Lord of the Rings*.

How will you create and use your secondary characters? You might want to create character biographies the way you did with your hero and villain. You should at least know what motivates them. How are they critical to the story, and why do they act the way they do?

Dialogue

Good dialogue propels the story. If you simply restate the obvious, then your dialogue is too "on the nose." After describing a fire-breathing dragon attacking a village, you don't need a character to say, "Look out! A dragon!" Instead, have him say something that also reveals his character. A hero might demonstrate his quick thinking by crying out, "Grab buckets! To the river!"

When writing dialogue speech verbs, a simple "he said" or "she said" is best. Too many beginning writers clutter their dialogue with unnecessary speech adverbs in order to show a character's emotions: *"Hand over the prince or face your doom," the knight said angrily.* So, what's so bad about "angrily"? It's much better to *show* action instead of using an adverb. For example: *The knight lowered the visor of his helm, then unsheathed his sword. "Hand over the prince or face your doom," he said.* Even though the writer simply used the word "said," the knight's angry tone is unmistakable.

Start a dialogue notebook. Write down speech you overhear at home, during lunch hour, or at the mall. You'll quickly discover that real speech is very different from written dialogue. Real speech often overlaps, and is filled with "ums," "ers," and "likes." Written dialogue should not mimic real speech; real speech on the page quickly becomes tedious.

Be wary of using the flowing, archaic language of medieval times. Most writers can't make this sound natural, and the dialogue seems stilted. Worse, it's tiresome to read. If ye do insist on scribing like this, thou mayest come to regret it.

PLOTS

"Fiction is a lie, and good fiction is the truth inside the lie."
—Stephen King

Planning a piece of fiction, especially a long piece like a novel, can be a daunting task. It becomes more manageable if you break it down into smaller parts. You've probably already learned in school that fiction has three key elements: a beginning, middle, and an end. That seems simple enough. These are sometimes referred to as Acts I, II, and III. Acts I and III (the beginning and end) are critical pieces of the story, but are relatively short. Act II holds the guts of the story, where the majority of the action takes place.

The beginning of a story is called the "hook." How do you best capture your readers' interest? Many authors, surprisingly, don't start at the beginning. Instead, their books start with a bang, right in the middle of the action, with the hero embroiled in an exciting scene. Only after the scene's action is resolved do we take a step back and reveal the major characters and setting. Remember, character is action. By starting with an action scene, we automatically learn something about the main character.

Three Key Elements of Fiction

Act I - Beginning— Introduction

Act II - Middle—Rising Action

Act III - End—Falling Action/Resolution

To Outline or Not?

Many writers create outlines of their story, right down to a scene-by-scene description of the action and each character's part in it. Sometimes authors use notecards, which can be shuffled around until all the scenes are arranged just right.

Other authors shun outlines. They start with an idea, add a strong character or two, and then let their storytelling sense guide them along the way. These authors argue that rigid outlines stifle creativity.

So, who's right? They both are. Great works of fiction have been written using both methods. But be warned that people who don't use outlines usually have to go back and do much more editing and revising after their first drafts are finished. Outlines provide a nice roadmap for beginning writers. Don't think of an outline as a rigid pathway; you can make changes along the way, and you probably will. But at least you've got a guide to help steer your story toward a satisfying conclusion.

Hero's Journey

After the beginning, how do you establish the plot and tie it all together? In *The Hero With a Thousand Faces*, author Joseph Campbell described patterns that are common to almost all works of fiction. They form a structure that authors use to tell the same basic tale, a story about a hero who goes on a quest to find a prize and bring it back to his or her tribe.

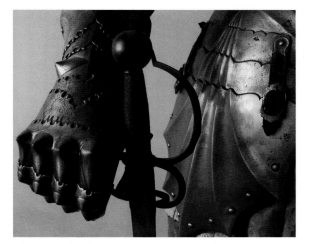

Above: A classic plot sends a hero on a quest to find a prize and bring it back.

Some writers think it's useful to keep this "hero's journey" in mind as they dream up their own stories. Of course, you don't have to rigidly follow the structure. It is merely a guide. But if you really study the books and movies you enjoy, you'll discover many of the following elements hidden within.

Act I

The Ordinary World

This section introduces the hero before the adventure begins. Typical fantasy stories show the hero in his or her "normal" world, before a creeping evil upsets the balance of all things. Time spent in the ordinary world allows the writer to identify what the hero wants, and what's at stake.

Above: When Harry Potter finds out he is a wizard, his whole world changes.

The Call to Adventure

This is where some sort of event happens that gets the story moving. There may be a message or temptation that calls your hero to act. The message is often delivered by a type of character, or archetype, called a herald, or a wise old man or woman.

Crossing the Threshold

This is the point where the hero makes a decision (or a decision is made for him), and he's thrown into the adventure. A critical event called a plot point occurs. The hero's world is threatened, or changed, and it's up to

Above: On a stormy night, Harry leaves his muggle relatives to seek adventure.

the hero to make things right. In fantasy stories, the stakes are high. If the hero fails in his or her quest, evil will forever rule the land.

Engage Your Senses

Russian novelist Anton Chekhov once said, "Don't tell me the moon is shining; show me the glint of light on broken glass." Use all your senses. Is there a hint of sweetness to the air, or is it stale? What sound does the wind make when it blows through a darkened woods? Show, don't tell.

Act II

Tests and Conflict

Act II is for testing the hero. What allies does she meet? What enemies? Who is the chief villain, and what are his goals? Does our hero act alone, or does she gather a group together, a posse?

Act II is a series of rising actions and mini-climaxes. In real life, events happen in seemingly random order. But in a good story, each event the hero encounters is connected, leading to the next ordeal.

The Crisis

The crisis is a point in the story where the hero faces her most fearsome test yet, perhaps even enduring a brush with death. It's the "dragging the hero through the gutter" scene, where the hero's faith in herself is put to the ultimate test. Then the hero makes a realization, or figures out a puzzle, and sets off for the final conflict.

Above: Harry is struck with searing pain when he comes face-to-face with evil.

Act III

The Final Struggle

This is the point in the story where the hero uses everything he's learned and faces the ultimate test. In many fantasy stories, the conflict becomes a physical action; the final struggle is a fight of some kind, using a combination of physical skills and magic learned during the quest.

Above: After many challenges, Harry faces the ultimate conflict. Can his skills and magic overcome the growing evil powers of Lord Voldemort?

Above: Harry is introduced to the powers of his magic wand.

Using Magic

Magic is a critical part of fantasy stories. Wizards, warlocks, witches—what's the point of including them in your fantasy story if they don't eventually use their magic? The trouble with magic is that if it is too powerful, then the actions of the characters become useless; we stop caring. If an all-powerful wizard can simply snap his fingers and make everything right, then what's the point of telling the story?

Make sure the magic in your fantasy world is both consistent and limited. You can be as imaginative and creative as you want with your magic, but it has to make sense within the fantasy setting. For example, perhaps magic wands only work when the tide is high (because of the moon's gravitational pull). Or maybe a wizard can cast powerful spells, but they're so exhausting that he instantly goes into a deep sleep for hours afterwards.

It's always best if your character wins the conflict on his own, especially if he uses skills learned during the course of the story. Beware of having another character swoop in to save the day. This kind of ending is called a *deus ex machina*, a Latin phrase that means "machine of the gods." In some ancient Greek plays, a cage with an actor portraying a god inside was lowered onto the stage, where he would miraculously solve the hero's seemingly hopeless problems. You've probably read books or watched movies where a similar event happened: an unexpected person or situation arises and saves the day. This is what some critics refer to as a contrived ending. Don't resort to this! You've spent the whole story building up your hero with new wisdom and skills. Let him save himself. Otherwise, what's the point of telling your story?

The Return

In many stories, the hero finally returns to his normal world. He brings back a prize, a symbolic magical elixir that benefits his people. Maybe it's gold, or medicine, or simply wisdom. But whatever the prize, what really matters is how the hero has changed (or didn't change) during his epic journey.

Above: Harry takes the train back to his muggle (non-magical) relatives.

REWRITING

"It is perfectly okay to write garbage—as long as you edit brilliantly."

—C.J. Cherryh

So, you finally finished your story. Congratulations! Whether it's a short story or a novel, you've achieved something most people only dream of. Take a step back, celebrate a little, and then get ready for more work, because there's a truth that you will soon discover: writing is rewriting. Editing your work is a crucial part of the entire process.

Don't edit yourself until you've cranked all the way through your story. If you edit while you write, you'll find things you don't like. It will stifle your creativity as you struggle to make things "perfect." Get that first draft finished, then go back and edit.

First, set your story aside for a couple weeks, or at least a few days. Amazingly, with fresh eyes you'll catch mistakes that snuck under your radar the first time around. Your second draft will be better than your first. Your third draft will be an even bigger improvement. Edit and polish your story until it shines. How many drafts do you need? It depends on the story. Some authors do a dozen drafts, others are content with only one or two drafts of editing after the first. You're done when you know in your heart that you've written your story to the very best of your ability.

If you're a writer, then you know the importance of good grammar and spelling. There's no substitute for carefully proofing the story with your own two eyes.

Examine your plot. Are the characters well formed? Do they grow and change? Most important, is your hero likeable? Does the hero have traits we admire? Can we identify with him or her? Do we care if the hero succeeds?

What about the beginning of your book? Does it grab the reader by the throat and never let go?

Are there scenes or events that are really necessary to push the story forward? Be honest with yourself. Be ruthless. Your story will be stronger the tighter you make it. Always, always remember your readers.

Keep your paragraphs short.

When appropriate, use active verbs instead of passive verbs. Instead of "The goblin was struck by the wizard's fireball," try "The wizard's fireball struck the goblin." See how much more immediate and interesting that simple change made the sentence?

Make sure you keep one point of view per scene.

Read your dialogue out loud. Does it sound natural? Does each character have his or her own "voice"?

Left: Use active verbs, such as, "The wizard controlled the earth and sky."

GET PUBLISHED

"The reason 99 percent of all stories written are not bought by editors is very simple. Editors never buy manuscripts that are left on the closet shelf at home."

—John Campbell

Your story is written and edited—now what? There are many web sites that publish work by young writers. Do an Internet search for "fantasy webzines" to find good sites. Many of these web sites are also terrific places to learn your craft, with free advice from established authors. You won't get paid much (if anything), but it's a way to get your work seen by an enthusiastic audience.

Or, you could start your own web site and publish online yourself. Some authors post the first chapter or two of their books as a free download, then charge a small fee if the reader wants more. Other authors post their entire work online, happy just to receive reader feedback.

Other Options:

- School newspapers or yearbooks. These publications are always hungry for material.
- Local, regional, or national creative-writing contests.
- Creative-writing clubs and workshops. These are a great way to get feedback from other writers. They also give you practice in critiquing others' work, which will improve your own writing.

- Local newspapers and magazines are always looking for new talent, especially if they can get it for cheap. Still, you have to start somewhere, and it's a way to get your work read by a large audience.
- Self publish. With today's page-layout software, it's easier than ever to create your own publication. Make copies for friends and family.

Publishers

If you are determined to have your story accepted by an established book publisher, first make sure your manuscript is ready. A clean, typewritten, double-spaced, mistake-free manuscript will go a long way in making your story stand out from all the rest. There are many "writer's guide" publications, some available at your library, you can use to research fantasy markets. They can also tell you how to write a query letter. Put your manuscript in a self-addressed stamped envelope (SASE), wish yourself luck, and mail it off. But please don't sit around waiting for a reply. Keep reading and writing!

Final Thoughts

If you receive a rejection letter, don't despair. Everybody gets them! Remember, the publisher isn't rejecting *you*, only your story. Maybe your writing isn't strong enough just yet. Or maybe your writing is fine, but the publisher isn't buying stories like yours at this time. Trends come and go in the marketplace, but don't try to write what you think publishers are looking for. By the time you finish your book, the fickle public will have moved on to the Next Big Thing. Simply write what you love, and the rest will follow.

You have the gift of storytelling. Sometimes you just need good timing and a little bit of luck. But remember, the more persistent you are, the luckier you'll get. Keep writing!

ADVICE FROM FANTASY WRITERS

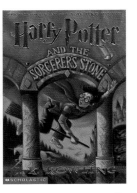

"Read as much as you can. I think that there is nothing as important, because that will really show you what makes good writing in your opinion. Obviously, it's very subjective. You will probably go through a phase when you imitate your favorite writers and I think that is necessary and a good learning process. After that, you just have to accept it takes a phenomenal amount of perseverance... you probably will not like 90 percent of what you write, and then one day you write a single page you like and build on that."

J.K. Rowling (1965-)

J.K. Rowling is a British writer best known for her series of best-selling books about Harry Potter, the boy wizard. The adventures of Harry and his friends at Hogwarts School of Witchcraft and Wizardry have together sold more than 400 million books worldwide. Rowling got the idea for the first book, *Harry Potter and the Sorcerer's Stone*, while riding a train to London in 1990. She finished the manuscript five years later. After several publishers turned down the book, she finally landed a contract. The book became a huge hit, spawning six sequels and a series of Hollywood blockbusters.

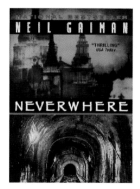

"I wanted a hero who was not a hero. I wanted somebody who was a little bit everybody, someone who was not the kind of person who would make the list if you were putting together a hero roster, but who was going to get by on essentially a good heart and good intentions, which were going to get him into deep trouble, but perhaps get him out again as well."

—Neil Gaiman discusses creating the hero of *Neverwhere*

Neil Gaiman (1960-)

The *Dictionary of Literary Biography* lists fantasy author Neil Gaiman as one of the top writers living and working today. His range of creativity is breathtaking: novels, short stories, comic books, journalism, song lyrics, drama, and screenplays. He was born in 1960 in England, where he grew up. Today he lives and works in the United States, near Minneapolis, Minnesota, in what he calls "my big Addams Family house." Gaiman has won many awards for his writing. Recent books include *Anansi Boys*, *Coraline*, and *The Graveyard Book*.

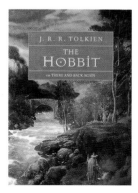

"What really happens is that the story-maker proves a successful 'sub-creator.' He makes a Secondary World which your mind can enter. Inside it, what he relates is 'true': it accords with the laws of that world. You therefore believe it, while you are, as it were, inside. The moment disbelief arises, the spell is broken; the magic, or rather art, has failed. You are then out in the Primary World again, looking at the little abortive Secondary World from outside."

J.R.R. Tolkien (1892—1973)

J.R.R. Tolkien was an English writer and university professor who penned the fantasy novels *The Hobbit* and *The Lord of the Rings* trilogy. Tolkien's fictional world of Middle-earth is a fantastic collection of landscapes, invented languages, and unforgettable characters, including Gandalf the wizard and the hobbits Bilbo and Frodo Baggins. Some believe that the key to Tolkien's success was his ability to retreat into his fictional world, which existed only in his mind. He *believed* in Middle-earth, and this vision came out in his writing.

HELPFUL READING

- *A Writer's Guide to Fantasy Literature* edited by Philip Martin

- *How to Write Tales of Horror, Fantasy & Science Fiction* edited by J.N. Williamson

- *The Writer's Journey: Mythic Structure for Writers* by Christopher Vogler

- *The Hero With a Thousand Faces* by Joseph Campbell

- *Stein on Writing* by Sol Stein

- *Self-Editing for Fiction Writers* by Renni Browne and Dave King

- *Writing Dialogue* by Tom Chiarella

- *Building Believable Characters* by Marc McCutcheon

- *Zen in the Art of Writing* by Ray Bradbury

- *The Elements of Style* by William Strunk, Jr., and E.B. White

- *The Transitive Vampire* by Karen Elizabeth Gordon

- *Roget's Super Thesaurus* by Marc McCutcheon

- *2009 Writer's Market* by Robert Brewer

- *Jeff Herman's Guide to Publishers, Editors, & Literary Agents 2009* by Jeff Herman

GLOSSARY

Antagonist — Often called the villain, the antagonist is an important character who tries to keep the hero from accomplishing his or her goal.

Archetype — A type of character that often appears in stories. Archetypes have special functions that move the story along, such as providing the hero with needed equipment or knowledge.

Backstory — The background and history of a story's characters and setting. When writing, it is good to know as much backstory as possible, even if most of it never appears in the final manuscript.

First-Person Viewpoint — The "I" viewpoint, which makes it seem as if the person telling the story is the one who experienced it first-hand. "I grabbed my sword and prepared to meet the gremlin invaders," is an example of first-person viewpoint.

Genre — A type, or kind, of a work of art. In literature, a genre is distinguished by a common subject, theme, or style. Some genres include science fiction, fantasy, mystery, and horror.

Hook — The beginning of a story, used to grab a reader's interest.

Plagiarism — To copy somebody else's work.

Point of View — The eyes, or viewpoint, through which we experience a story or scene.

Protagonist — A story's hero or main character. The protagonist propels the story.

Third-Person Viewpoint — A detached, neutral point of view in which the story is told by an all-seeing narrator. "Sir John grabbed his sword. Were those gremlins he'd heard in the hallway?" is an example of third-person viewpoint.

INDEX